Cu

# MIGHTY MOUNTAINS

— ✦ The facts and the fables ✦ —

Finn Bevan
Illustrated by Diana Mayo

W
FRANKLIN WATTS
LONDON • NEW YORK • SYDNEY

First published in 1997 by Watts Books
96 Leonard Street, London EC2A 4RH

Franklin Watts Australia
14 Mars Road
Lane Cove
NSW 2066

Series editor: Rachel Cooke
Art director: Robert Walster
Designer: Mo Choy
Picture research: Sarah Moule

A CIP catalogue record for this book
is available from the British Library.

ISBN 0 7496 2549 X

Dewey Classification 398.23

Printed in Singapore
Picture acknowledgements:
**AKG Photo** p. 6 (Kunstehistorisches Museum, Vienna)
**Ancient Art & Architecture Collection** p. 11
**Bruce Coleman** p. 26 (Paul R. Wilkinson)
**Werner Forman Archive** p. 27 (Private Collection, Prague)
**Robert Harding Picture Library** p. 24
**Helenic Literary and Historical Archives Society** p. 7
**Impact Photos** p. 20 (Thierry Bouzac)
**Panos Pictures** p. 17 (Mervyn T. Patterson)
**Tony Stone Images** p. 10 (Alan Kearney), 12 (Allan Bramley)

# Contents

✦

# Explaining the Earth

From the highest mountains to the deepest caves, the natural features of the Earth's landscape have a special importance for people all over the world. They have formed a focus for their beliefs and religions and, to explain their significance, people have created stories and myths. These fabulous fables tell not only how the natural world came to be but also how it affects and shapes people's lives.

*In Hindu legend, mountains were once flying elephants.*

## Mighty Mountains

Because of their great height, age and awe-inspiring appearance, mountains have always played a part in people's beliefs. In many ancient cultures, mountains are seen as the centre of the universe, where all life was created.

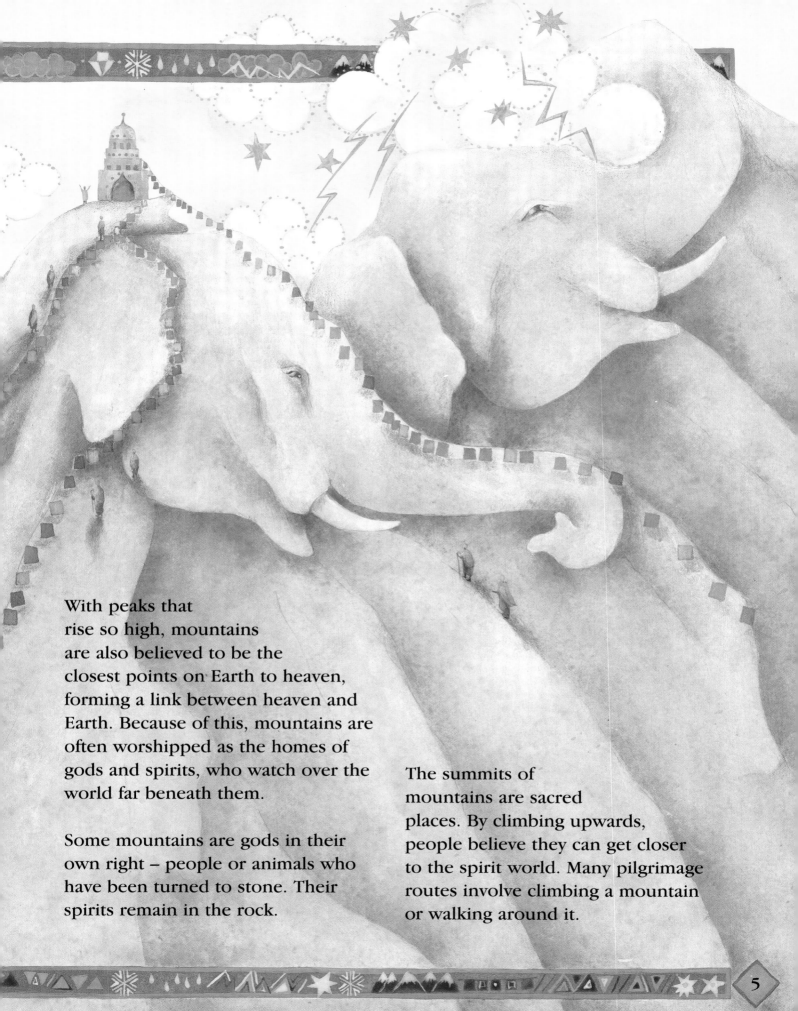

With peaks that rise so high, mountains are also believed to be the closest points on Earth to heaven, forming a link between heaven and Earth. Because of this, mountains are often worshipped as the homes of gods and spirits, who watch over the world far beneath them.

Some mountains are gods in their own right – people or animals who have been turned to stone. Their spirits remain in the rock.

The summits of mountains are sacred places. By climbing upwards, people believe they can get closer to the spirit world. Many pilgrimage routes involve climbing a mountain or walking around it.

# Home of the Gods

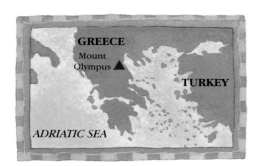

**M**ount Olympus is the highest mountain in Greece. It rises 2,917 m above sea level. Remote and snow covered for much of the year, but magnificently beautiful, it is no wonder that the people of Ancient Greece thought it a suitable home for their gods.

## Who Were the Olympians?

The Olympians were the gods who ruled the universe from their home on Mount Olympus. They were the most important of the many gods worshipped by the Ancient Greeks. The gods were like humans in appearance and character, but they were also immortal – they lived for ever. We know the myths that surrounded them through Ancient Greek writers.

### Zeus, Hera and Their Children

Zeus was the king of the gods, and the ruler of the heavens. He kept control by use of his mighty thunderbolts. Hera, his wife and sister, was the goddess of marriage and women. They had several children: two of them, Ares, god of war, and Hephaestus, god of fire, were also Olympians.

*The head of Zeus*

Zeus    Hera    Ares    Hephaestus    Poseidon    Hades    Hestia

## Brothers and Sisters

Zeus had two brothers: Poseidon, god of the sea, and Hades, god of the underworld, the kingdom of the dead. He also had two sisters who lived with him on Mount Olympus: Hestia, goddess of the hearth and home, and Demeter, goddess of plants and farming. Another Olympian was Aphrodite, Zeus's half-sister and the goddess of love and beauty.

## Zeus's Other Children

The remaining Olympians were all children of Zeus but had other mothers than Hera. Artemis was the moon goddess and Apollo was god of the sun. Hermes was the messenger of the gods and Athena, the goddess of wisdom and war, was born from Zeus's head after he swallowed her mother!

*Another of Zeus's sons, Dionysus (pictured right on a Greek drinking cup), was the very popular god of wine. He became an Olympian when Hestia resigned her place.*

Demeter  Aphrodite  Artemis  Apollo  Hermes  Athena  Dionysus

*This is the story of the birth of Hephaestus, the god's smith. He worked in his forge in the heart of Mount Olympus, deep underground.*

◆

There was much rejoicing in the gods' palace, high on Mount Olympus.

Hera, queen of the gods, had given birth to a son. But had the celebrations started too soon?

"Let me hold my son," Hera demanded. Her attendants seemed nervous. "Bring him here," she insisted. "Let me gaze on his beautiful face."

Reluctantly, a nurse placed a squalling bundle into Hera's arms. The goddess eagerly pulled back the shawl to see her new baby. Her scream could be heard in the foothills of Olympus.

"A monster, a monster! Oh Zeus, our son is uglier than a one-eyed cyclops!" Before anyone could stop her, Hera leapt from her bed, ran to the balcony and threw the baby over the edge.

"A creature so hideous is not fit to stay on Mount Olympus," she declared.

Her attendants said nothing. After all, who could argue with the queen of the gods?

Down and down the baby fell, passed rocky outcrops and through misty clouds, burning bright with immortality. Finally, he crashed headlong into the sea, but, before the waves closed over his head, a pair of gentle arms caught him. They were the arms of a sea nymph, and she and her sister named the baby Hephaestus or "dayshine".

For nine long years, Hephaestus stayed in the sea nymphs' grotto. He was still ugly but grew enormously strong, with power over fire and the gift of craftsmanship. His powerful hands wrought silver and gold into jewels and ornaments more exquisite than anything seen before. They also forged the means for revenge on his mother.

One day, Hera received a gift from her son – a fabulous golden throne. She sat on it with great delight. But when she tried to get up again, she found she was tied down with invisible bands. No one but Hephaestus could set her free. And he would only do so if she admitted her cruelty towards him.

Hera was caught: at last she acknowledged her misdeeds and welcomed her son back to Mount Olympus where he lived in a palace of glittering bronze. Some say you can still hear the blows of a hammer echoing deep within the mountain. Hephaestus is at work, forging beautiful, delicate gifts for the gods.

# Himalayan Heaven

Stretching for more than 2,400 km across northern India, and into Pakistan, Tibet, Nepal and Bhutan, are the Himalayas, the highest mountains in the world. According to Hindu myth, history began in the Himalayas and all people, languages and religions were created there. The mountains themselves were once flying elephants until the Hindu god, Indra, cut off their wings.

## The Jewel of the Snows

Among the Himalayan peaks of western Tibet, stands Mount Kailash. Known locally as *Kang Rinpoche*, the "Jewel of the Snows", it is 6,714 m high and shaped like a giant, ice-covered cone. At its feet lie two sacred lakes, Mansarovar, representing the forces of light, and Rakastal, representing the forces of darkness.

*Sunset transforms the Himalayas into a magical world. No wonder myths of jewel-covered mountains grew up.*

## Shiva's Palace

Mount Kailash is worshipped by Hindus as the home of the great god, Shiva, and his wife, the goddess Parvati.

### *Shiva and Parvati*

Shiva is the destroyer of evil in the universe. He is often shown sitting on Mount Kailash, deep in meditation. In statues and sculptures, Shiva often holds a trident, the symbol of destruction. On his forehead are three horizontal stripes and the third eye of knowledge. Parvati is Shiva's beautiful wife, and the daughter of Himavan, god of the Himalayas.
She is worshipped both as a gentle mother goddess and as Durga, goddess of war.

*A 10th-century carving of Shiva and Parvati*

## Mountain Race

Mount Kailash is also sacred to Jains, Buddhists and followers of Bon, the ancient religion of Tibet. Legend says that the great Buddhist teacher, Milarepa, won a race up the mountain, beating the Bon priest Naro-Bonchung. Disgusted, Naro-Bonchung dropped his magic drum, leaving a long, vertical gash in the mountain's south face.

## The Centre of the Universe

For Hindus and Jains, Mount Kailash is also believed to be the mythical Mount Meru which stands at the very centre of the universe, between Heaven and Earth. It is surrounded by seven continents and seven seas, and its four faces are made of crystal, lapis lazuli, gold and ruby.

"There is a shining mountain called Meru. Its blazing golden peaks outshine the sun. The gods live on its glittering, golden slopes but mortal men cannot approach. The mountain top reaches to heaven. Its fabulous slopes are studded with jewels and magic wishing-trees. Here the gods sit to take counsel."
From the Hindu scripture, *The Mahabharata*

## A Place of Pilgrimage

Because of its sacredness, Mount Kailash is a place of pilgrimage for Hindus and Buddhists. Pilgrims walk in a 50-km circuit, called a *parikrama*, around the mountain's base. The circuit takes 2 to 3 days to complete on foot. For Buddhists, performing the *parikrama* once is enough to wipe away all their sins. Performing it 108 times allows them to reach *nirvana*, or salvation.

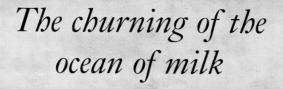
*This is a Hindu story which tells of the struggle between the Devas, the lesser gods, and Asuras, the demons, to win the elixir of everlasting life. It involves two mythical mountains, Mount Meru and Mount Mandara.*

◆

At the beginning of time, there was an ocean of milk and everything came from it – the land, the sky, light and darkness, fire and fruits, and *amrita*, the elixir of life. From their lofty home on Mount Meru, the great gods looked down and pondered how to win the elixir for themselves. "We'll let the Devas and Asuras churn the ocean," they decided, "just like you churn milk to make butter. And instead of butter, we'll have *amrita*."

The Devas and Asuras had to find a churning stick strong enough for such a mighty task. So they went to the great mountain, Mandara, and they pulled it up by its roots. They placed it on the back of a tortoise, "This can be our churning stick," they said.

With the gigantic serpent king, Vasuki, wound around the mountain as their rope, the Devas and Asuras began to churn the ocean of milk. The Devas pulled at one end; the Asuras at the other, sending Mount Mandara into a spin.

Smoke and fire poured out of Vasuki's mouth;
the trees on Mount Mandara toppled over and caught fire.
But, slowly, and surely, the ocean of milk began to foam and froth.
First, it turned to thick, creamy butter. With a last desperate effort, the
Devas and Asuras churned some more. And finally, they had their hearts'
desire – a gleaming white bowl of *amrita*, the elixir of everlasting life.

But, as the great god, Vishnu, reached down to take the bowl and
carry it back to Mount Meru, Rahu, the most evil Asura of all, snatched
it from him and flew away. Woe betide the world if Rahu lived forever!

Quick as a flash, Vishnu took action.

Before Rahu could
take more than a sip, Vishnu cut off
his head with a stroke. Rahu's body crashed to
Earth – but his terrible head stayed where it was in the
sky, roaring and howling in pain. A tiny drop of *amrita* had
reached Rahu's throat, so his head could never die.

A terrible battle now broke out between the Devas and Asuras, the
gods and the demons. Thousands lay dead and dying before the Asuras
were beaten. The gods put Mount Mandara back in its proper place. At
last they could return home to Mount Meru.

With great rejoicing, the gods divided the *amrita* amongst themselves.
Now they were immortal and could live forever on the gleaming heights
of Mount Meru.

The only Asura to survive the battle was Rahu's head, destined forever
to chase the Moon across the night sky. Every month, he catches and
swallows it and the Moon wanes. Then the Moon escapes and, before
Rahu can catch it once more, it grows again,
reaching its full shining circle.

# Hills of the Lord

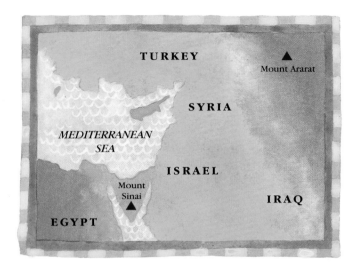

Two great mountains of the Middle East, Mount Ararat in Turkey and Mount Sinai in Egypt, are sacred to Jews and Christians alike. Both are mentioned in the Old Testament of the Bible. Both are believed to be the sites of amazing events which happened thousands of years ago.

## Mount Ararat

Mount Ararat lies in eastern Turkey. Its two peaks, Great Ararat (5,165 m) and Little Ararat (3,925 m) were formed long ago by volcanic eruptions. Great Ararat has a vast glacier down its northern side and, in winter, is capped with snow. Despite the snow, the region is very dry and most of the mountain is bare of trees.

### The Ark Comes to Rest

According to the Bible, Noah's Ark came to rest on the summit of Mount Ararat after the terrible flood which God sent to punish the world. The mountain was the only land high enough to rise above the floodwaters. Legend says that Noah built an altar and planted a vineyard on the mountain slope to give thanks for being saved.

# Mount Sinai

The Bible tells how Moses was chosen by God to lead the Israelites out of slavery in Egypt. As they travelled, God summoned Moses to a high mountain. It was here that God revealed his will to Moses, in the form of the Ten Commandments. These are still followed by both Jews and Christians. The mountain where this extraordinary event took place was Mount Sinai, a 2,400-m peak in Egypt. It is also called *Jebel Musa*, the Mountain of Moses.

*Mount Sinai is part of a barren, desert mountain range.*

### In Moses' Footsteps

For centuries, Mount Sinai has been an important place of pilgrimage. Of the several pathways winding up the mountain, the most famous is called "The Path of Our Lord Moses". It takes three hours to climb up and down its 8,000 steps.

# Moses and the Ten Commandments

*This is the story told in the Bible of how Moses received the Ten Commandments from God on the summit of Mount Sinai.*

◆

Three months after leaving Egypt and their lives of slavery behind, the Israelites came to the desert of Sinai. The journey had been long and hard, and the people were tired and frightened. Moses told them to pitch their camp at the foot of the mountain. Then he climbed up the mountain to pray to God.

"Tell the people not to be afraid," God told Moses. "I will lead them safely to the Promised Land. In three days' time, I will appear to you all from the top of this mountain. Be ready."

So the Israelites waited patiently for three days to pass. When the third day came, the top of the mountain lay wreathed in thick clouds. Then the sky erupted with peals of thunder and jagged flashes of lightning. A trumpet sounded so loudly that the people trembled with fear. Before their eyes, God came down on to the mountain in the form of fire. He called Moses to him.

There on the mountain, God gave Moses the Ten Commandments, to guide and keep his chosen people. And he wrote them down on tablets of stone. This is what they said:

1  I AM THE LORD YOUR GOD

2  DO NOT WORSHIP ANY OTHER GOD

3  DO NOT TAKE MY NAME IN VAIN

4  KEEP THE SABBATH HOLY FOR PRAYER AND REST

5  RESPECT YOUR FATHER AND MOTHER

6  DO NOT KILL ANYONE

7  DO NOT COMMIT ADULTERY

8  DO NOT STEAL

9  DO NOT ACCUSE PEOPLE WRONGLY

10  DO NOT BE ENVIOUS OF OTHER PEOPLE'S BELONGINGS

Then Moses came down from the mountain and told the people what God had said.

"We will do everything the Lord has said," they replied.

Then God told them to build a golden chest in which to keep the tablets of the law, and a temple where they could come and worship him. Then, after many trials and tribulations, many mishaps and adventures, he led them out of the wilderness and into the Promised Land.

# African Ancestors

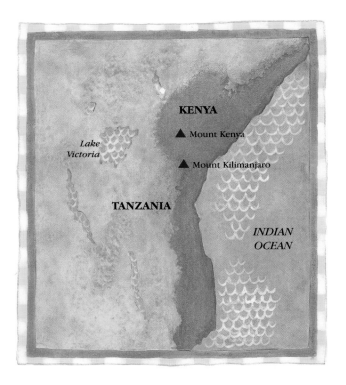

In African mythology, mountains are special places. For people believe that their earliest ancestors came from the mountains and spread out all over Africa. The two highest mountains in Africa are Mount Kilimanjaro (5,895 m) in Tanzania and Mount Kenya (5,199 m). They are also the most sacred. Despite lying close to the Equator, both mountains are capped with snow all year round and have permanent glaciers on their slopes.

## Mount Kenya

Mount Kenya is an extinct volcano. Strange looking plants, such as giant groundsel and lobelias, grow on its lower slopes. The mountain is sacred to the local Kikuyu people who believe it to be the home of God. For this reason, they always build their own homes with the doors facing the mountain. They also turn towards the mountain to pray.

One of the local names for Mount Kenya is *Kirinyaga* which means "the black and white peak spotted like ostrich feathers"!

# The Kikuyu find a home

*This story tells of the origins of the Kikuyu people of Kenya and how the tribe grew from one family into many.*

◆

When the world was still young, God, the creator, made himself a great mountain as a sign of his wonder and as a place where he could rest from his labours. This was Mount Kenya. From his mountain, God watched over the world and the people below.

Now God had three sons – Kamba, Masai and Gikuyu. One day, he summoned Gikuyu, the father of the Kikuyu people, to the top of his mountain and showed him the land, with its rivers, valleys, forests and animals, and all the things that God had made.

Right in the middle was a cluster of fig trees.

"Make that place your home," he told Gikuyu.

When Gikuyu reached the place, he found it to be a very fine spot indeed. God also sent him a beautiful wife, called Moombi. The happy couple had nine pretty daughters but, secretly, Gikuyu wanted a son. So he went back to the great mountain and asked God to help him.

"Don't worry, Gikuyu," God told him. "You will have a son. This is what you must do. Take a lamb and a kid, and sacrifice them by the great tree at the foot of the mountain. Then pour the blood over the tree trunk and offer the meat to God."

Gikuyu did exactly as God told him. Then he went home to his wife and daughters. When he reached the fig trees, he saw, to his joy, that nine young men had joined his family. How proud he was to have not one but nine fine sons! A great feast was held in celebration. Gikuyu, his wife and their 18 children ate, drank and made merry. Then they went to sleep.

Some time later, the day finally came for the young men to get married. Gikuyu offered them his daughters as wives, on one condition – they must all live together in the family home. They agreed.

And so the Kikuyu lived together in one group, helping each other with the ups and downs of life. And time passed and more babies were born. Soon the village by the fig trees became too small for everyone to live in. Some of the people moved into the forest and traded with the forest hunters for more land. And so they spread out from the plains to the forests. But they never moved far from the great mountain where God had made his home. And they never will...

# Fire Mountain

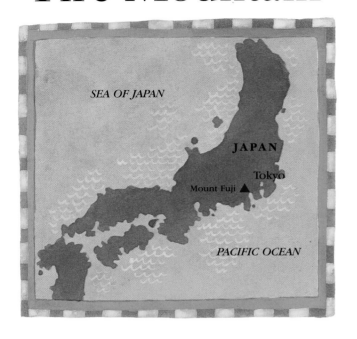

SEA OF JAPAN

JAPAN

Tokyo

Mount Fuji ▲

PACIFIC OCEAN

Towering 3,776 m into the air, the famous volcanic cone of Mount Fuji can be seen for hundreds of miles around. Japan's highest and most famous mountain, it has become a symbol of the whole country. In Japanese, the mountain is called *Fujisan* which means "Fire Mountain". It last erupted in 1707. Its massive crater once held a vast lake but is now filled with snow.

## Shinto Spirits

In the ancient Shinto religion of Japan, mountains, trees and rivers are all worshipped as the homes of gods, or as gods in their own right. These gods are called *kami*. Mount Fuji is the home of a goddess called Sengen-sama whose shrine stands on the summit, and of the fire god, who causes the mountain to erupt.

## Climbing to Heaven

Mount Fuji is sacred to Shintoists and Buddhists alike. Thousands of pilgrims climb the mountain every year, to gain protection against ill fortune.

*An aerial photograph of Mount Fuji's crater*

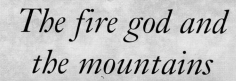

# The fire god and the mountains

*This is the story of how the death of the fire god gave life to the gods of the mountains.*

◆

The first two people to appear on Earth were Izanagi and his wife, Izanami. They stood on the Floating Bridge of Heaven, took a long, jewelled spear and stirred the swirling waters below. A drop of water fell from the spear and created an island in the sea.

"What a beautiful place," Izanagi said. "Let us make our home there." They settled down to live happily ever after. And their many children became the gods and islands.

Then disaster struck. Izanami had another child – the fire god, but his birth burned her so badly she died. In his grief and rage, Izanagi picked up his sword and cut off the fire god's head. Then he chopped his body into five pieces. Each piece took on a life of its own: the first piece became the chief god and lord of the mountains. The second and third became the gods of the lower mountain slopes. The fourth became the god of steep slopes, and the fifth the god of the mountain foot.

Although the fire god was dead, his spirit lived on. Many a time the water-goddess was called on to try to control him. But his temper was very terrible indeed. And, even today, when a mighty volcano begins to rumble and belch out smoke, it can mean just one thing – the fire god is angry, very angry indeed.

# Mountains of Dreamtime

To the Aborigines of Australia, all the features of the Earth, including mountains, are sacred. They were created by the ancestors thousands of years ago during a period called the Dreamtime. Two of the Aborigines' most sacred sites lie in central Australia. Both are dramatic masses of glowing red sandstone rock – the mighty *Uluru* (Ayers Rock) and *Katajuta* (the Olgas).

## The Great Pebble

The name *Uluru* means "great pebble", a good description of the great oval-shaped boulder which rises 380 m above the sand-dunes in the dry Australian desert. The base of the rock measures 9 km around and is pitted with caves, worn away by centuries of wind and weather. Many are decorated with paintings telling myths and stories from the Dreamtime.

In ancient times, *Uluru* was also the site of the most important waterhole for miles around. In the dry season, fights broke out among the tribes for its precious water.

*The giant pebble*, Uluru, *in the Australian desert*

## Many Heads

Some 30 km west of *Uluru* lies a jumble of 30 or so huge boulders, known to the Aborigines as *Katajuta*, or "many heads". Like *Uluru*, this is a sacred site of the Dreamtime and the home of the snake-spirit, Wanambi. It was also, in olden times, a ceremonial meeting place for the different Aborigine tribes.

*An Aboriginal painting of the Dreamtime*

## The Dreamtime

In Aborigine beliefs, the Dreamtime happened thousands of years ago, but is still with us today. Their ancestors travelled across Australia, shaping the landscape as they went, like footsteps left forever in the sand. Through their actions, they created the hills and waterholes, lakes and caves. Some travelled in human form; others as animals – kangaroos, snakes, lizards and birds. There are many stories and songs about their wanderings.

# The battle for Uluru

*This is the tragic story of how the landscape around Uluru was shaped and formed during the Dreamtime.*

◆

In the Dreamtime, thousands of years ago, two peace-loving tribes of snake-people, the Woma and Kunia, left their camp in the east and journeyed west to a great sandhill by the Uluru waterhole. There they split into groups and set up camp. The women gathered seeds and roots while the men went hunting. Their bodies are the boulders by the sandhill.

Time passed by peacefully. Then one day, a group of poisonous snake-people came to the camp. Armed with spears, clubs and knives, they attacked the Kunia. The attackers remain as the trees around Uluru.

Not long before, a Kunia woman had given birth to a baby. Her body formed the caves in the rock. A jagged rock is her baby. She took the baby and walked towards the attackers, spitting out

darkness and death. Many fell down dead but the rest kept coming, shouting insults, while the rest of her people fled. Their tracks can be seen as layers in the rock.

When they reached the gorge, a young Kunia hero fought the enemy leader. Both were badly wounded, the Kunia hero worst of the two. As he crawled away to die, his body formed the bed of a stream and his blood the water in it.

His grief-stricken mother, Ingridi, gave a terrible scream and killed the enemy leader herself. In return, his brother killed Ingridi's daughter and her children. Her body is now a boulder, still with the holes made by the spear which killed her.

When Ingridi heard of her daughter's death, she killed herself and the rest of the snake-people by chanting the deadly song of darkness and death.

# Notes and Explanations

## Who's Who

ABORIGINES: The original inhabitants of Australia who arrived there thousands of years ago. The Aborigines traditionally lived as nomadic hunter-gatherers. To them, the land is sacred, given form and shape during the Dreamtime. Since the arrival of European settlers in Australia, the Aborigines have struggled to keep their culture alive and to safeguard their sacred landscape.

ANCIENT GREEKS: The people who lived in Greece from about 2,000 BC. Theirs was a highly advanced civilisation, famous for its art, literature, science and trade. Myths formed an important part of Ancient Greek religion, explaining the nature and exploits of the gods. We know these myths through the works of Ancient Greek writers such as the poet, Homer, who lived in about the 8th century BC.

BUDDHISTS: People who follow the teachings of Siddhartha Gautama who lived in India in the 6th century BC. Siddhartha sought a way out of life's sufferings. After years of fasting and meditation, he at last saw the truth and became known as the Buddha, or "awakened one".

CHRISTIANS: Followers of Jesus Christ, a preacher and teacher who lived 2,000 years ago in Palestine. Christians believe he is the Son of God. Jesus was sentenced to death for his beliefs and crucified on a cross. His disciples spread his message far and wide. Today there are about 200 million Christians, in every continent. Their holy book is the Bible.

HINDUS: Followers of the Hindu religion, which began in India some 4,500 years ago. About 80 per cent of Indians are Hindus. They believe in a wide variety of gods and in reincarnation (being born again after you die). The aim of a Hindu's life is to break free of the cycle of birth and rebirth, and gain salvation.

JEWS: There are about 14 million Jews living all over the world. They follow a religion which began some 4,000 years ago in the Middle East. According to Jewish law, anyone whose mother is Jewish is a Jew. Most Jews actively follow Judaism as a religion, though not all. The holy book of the Jews is the *Torah*, the first five books of the Jewish Bible.

KIKUYU: A farming people of northern Kenya who live on and around the lower slopes of Mount Kenya. There are about 3 million Kikuyu. Their ancestors are thought to have come from east Africa in the 16th century. The Kikuyu live in large clans, made up of smaller, family groups and ruled by a council of elders.

SHINTO: The ancient religion of Japan. Shintoists believe in spirits, called *kami*, which live in shrines and sacred places, including mountains, rivers and trees. Their most important *kami* is Amaterasu, the sun goddess. The Japanese royal family is believed to be directly descended from her.

# What's What
Strictly speaking, fables, legends and myths are all slightly different. But the three terms are often used to mean the same thing – a symbolic story or a story with a message.

FABLE: A short story, not based in fact, which often has animals as its central characters and a strong moral lesson to teach.

LEGEND: An ancient, traditional story based on supposed historical figures or events.

MYTH: A story which is not based in historical fact but which uses supernatural characters to explain natural phenomena, such as the weather, night and day, the rising tides and so on. Before the scientific facts were known, ancient people used myths to make sense of the world around them.

PILGRIMAGE: A journey made to a sacred place as an act of religious faith and devotion. Sacred places include natural sites, such as mountains and rivers, and places connected with the history of a religion, such as Jerusalem, where Jesus Christ was crucified.

# Where's Where
The map below shows where in the world the mountains named in this book are found.

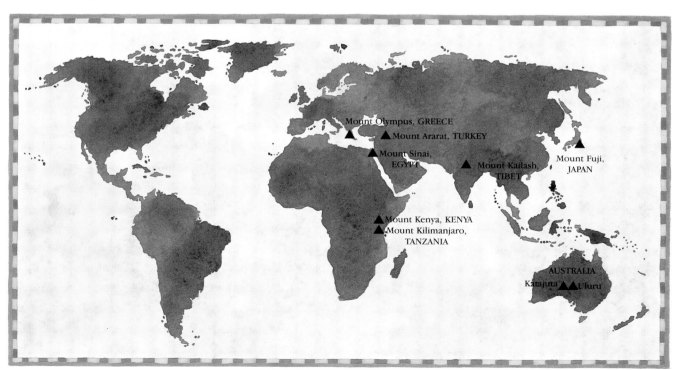

# Index